CW00927038

# EQUINOX

*To every heartbreak disguised as blessings*

The celestial event that marks a transition in seasons is called an "equinox" and it happens twice every year, upon the arrival of spring and autumn. The concept of an equinox, to me, is a symbol of inevitable change. In September, through the first few gusts of wind, the Autumnal Equinox greets us with the ominous reminder that a long winter is ahead. In March, the green begins to peek through the snow as the Vernal Equinox brings us sunnier days. Change, like Mother Nature, is not for or against you. It just *is*.

Each and every experience with loss and heartache inspires the metamorphosis of the person you will become.

I hope you remember to welcome the seasons that shape who you are.

*Parallel Lines*

I don't want your memories of me
to keep you warm at night,
I hope they burn behind your eyes.

You and I
are like parallel lines,
because now that we are here
alive and breathing,
happy and healed,
we will continue to live
but we will never touch.

*Clementine*

On an empty stomach
you'll always reach for her;
a low hanging fruit
is easy and safe,

but a smart man knows
that the best fruits ripen
at the top of trees;
closest to the sun
hardest to reach,
but always worth the climb.

## Toothache

You are the throbbing in my head,
the piercing ache my tongue loves
to brush over throughout the day,
shooting a pain into my
nerves the moment I
forget about you.

My mouth sinks
deeper and deeper
into your skin,
seeping streams of condensed milk.

You are the shiny sucrose coating
on a rotten soul.

I will always save room for you
and ignore every consequence
for strawberry jam lips.

## What It's Like to Love Somebody with Depression

You told me that your favorite season was Summer
and I began to envy the way dandelions sway
and disappear so easily into the wind, feeble and free.

I am wilting, rooted deep in misery
with bulky thorns that anyone would be foolish to
withstand.

Have you ever known a happy girl?

She is not a heavy burden,
she is light as a feather.
There is no sadness that plagues her,
only light in her eyes.
There is a gleam that radiates
and warms everyone around her.
She is not the gust of cold wind
that stings your cheeks and fingertips.
She reminds you of opening bedroom windows
in late May when the magnolias would grow
rampant.

Me,
I am the last petal to fall in Autumn.
It is only until the dead of my winter
that you will begin to miss the sun.
You reach out to me, but your hands are so cold.
I will not blame you for wanting to find Summer
elsewhere.

*Smoke and Mirrors*

I lost myself
in the arms of this magician
who, with a sleight of hand,
created illusions that clouded my mind.
He
whose tongue
could make self-control disappear.

Conjuring desire with his right hand
and distracting me from an old lover
holding the other.

You cannot say that you love a man
for who he is
if all he ever shows you are
deceitful projections of who he could be for you.

*Bathwater*

I would bathe
in your dirty water
if it meant
immersing myself
in all the things
that have been on you
before my lips and hands could;

the smell of desperation and
salt on your skin,
the amber and musk of
perfume that was never mine.
Help me understand what you have
chosen to rinse yourself clean from
and all the delicate things
our love has outlived.

I will stay until my fingers prune.

*Phantoms*

I often imagine her as a phantom,
slipping through windows
and lingering in the empty hallways
of your memory.
If you find yourself there again,
be careful, my love;
nostalgia will have you falling
more in love with the echoes
than the words.

But with my lips
I want to rewrite history
until her voice will sound
so distant in your recollection
that they are nothing more to you
than tinkering piano keys
playing softly in another room.

*Forever & Always*

With concern in your eyes
recognizing the suffering in mine
you pulled me close,
held my hands and asked me,
*"Is my love making you crazy?"*
and with silence as my answer, I remember
how hard you fought to hide the smirk
curling at the corner of your lips.

*"I have proven to you that I am a good man,"* you said.
*"why are you still afraid to love me?"*

But these are words
that others before me have
heard plenty times before;
how they were once used to
pacify her fervent paranoia
and help lay her head down at night
while you drove two hundred fifty miles
away from home just to lay
a different woman down on hotel sheets.
How all the promises you gave
these other women of forever and always
were just lullabies to help them drift off
soundly into a comatose state,
blissfully unaware
of all that you do in the dark.

I am trying to stay awake.

So if you ask me why your words do not comfort me, it is
only because I am afraid of how you have become so well
versed.

*There is a cosmic boom in my head, a loud thunder. Every move he makes causes a prickly sensation on my fingertips and my chest thuds in a malfunctioning, violent wash cycle. This sensation has happened to me in all the years I have loved him, and I still don't know why.*

*How to Grow Roses*

I was seven years old when I learned that soil and a seed could fertilize if given enough sunlight and attention, but it was my own obsessive eagerness to breathe life into something that caused me to drown my roots with water. I quickly learned that the muddy marsh could never be a suitable home to a life of any kind.

My mother warned me that this paradox will follow me in life outside of botany.

I was twenty-two when you told me that my love for control will leave lovers wilted and rotting, and, much like nature, love can thrive with or without my criticism or impatience.

You left me, and it was only until then that your love reminded me of the roses that could never grow.

-    *If you love something, let it bloom*

I COUNTED ALL THE FRECKLES ON HER CHEEKS
FELL IN LOVE WITH THE WAY HER NOSE SCRUNCHED
WHEN SHE LAUGHED

*It Came in Waves*

For a long time, I was at peace. I knew that I was finally safe, and that he was too far away to ever touch my body again. For all that, someone will mindlessly spill his name in conversation and then a cold crash will send a jolt down my spine, knocking the wind out of my lungs, and the fortified dams I have built to keep me safe will then break; the repressed memories begin to flood. Suddenly I am immersed and I can feel his soft breathing, goose bumps bloom behind my neck and limbs. There was a time I thought I would know him forever. Though he's nothing more than a memory now, in a strange and prideful way, he still exists to me after all these years.

*Your Willing Victim*

Just like how a lion will always choose a weak victim as their prey, you knew that it was easy to make anything seem glamorous to a nineteen-year-old. You were charismatic, hot-blooded with a temper like a coiled spring. I was young and hungry for any experience that was spiritually and mentally arousing. Your mystery was enigmatic, and I had an intense desire to know what hid in the depths of cloudy water. In hindsight I was the perfect prey, wasn't I? It was my vulnerability that made me an easy target. I was wide-eyed and naïve to every red flag, saw danger as if it was stimulating and fun. I could say that I misconstrued your violence as passion. I could say that I blamed it on the drinking.

But none of these conclusions saved me from the seething disappointment I felt for myself.

*Cowboy Killers*

I loved the way his charm spoke for him before he ever muttered a word, the pin drop silence whenever he told his stories, and the eruption of laughter echoing throughout the room.

In between sips of his cheap beer
and puffs from a Marlboro red cigarette,
he coos "I love you"
in an assuring and comforting way
before he exhales the smoke
from his lungs into my hair.

I didn't know it then,
but this will be
the smell that will
latch onto my memory
like a cancerous phenomenon
killing me from the inside.


-    *I smoke your brand of cigarettes*
*so that I may always have your lips*
*on mine.*

*The Taste of Blood*

Do not ask me for forgiveness
when I can still taste the blood
in my mouth.

Forgiveness is not what we need when
no amount of sugar can take away
the sharp tang of iron
at the tip of my tongue
whenever I say your name.

It is not amnesty that I want from you.
It's to forget you completely.

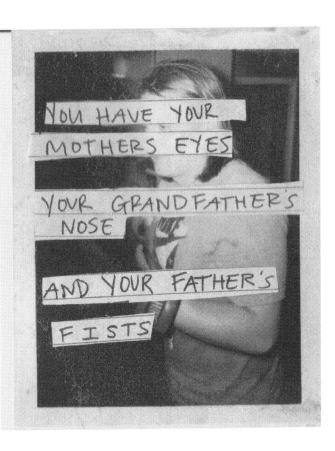

YOU HAVE YOUR
MOTHERS EYES
YOUR GRANDFATHER'S
NOSE
AND YOUR FATHER'S
FISTS

*Hopeless, Romantic*


Love brings a pendulum of emotions
swinging back and forth from
*suffering* to *impatiently longing*

*In Memoriam*

It's been so long
since I last visited you
in my daydreams
that I forgot where I buried
the softer version of you,
the one I held on to for years
that cost me
my mind
and my youth.

But whenever I feel the need to
dig you back out,
I will remember
the white of your knuckles
and how you always left things uglier
after touching them,
the craters in the drywall,
how your eyes are no longer
gold-speckled and mossy
like spring foliage
but instead
reptilian
and
evil,
the blood in my mouth
dripping, forming
peculiar patterns onto my jeans.

Now, my heart
no longer breaks for you.
I practice mourning you
in acceptance instead.
I allow my yearning to pass
like fleeting storms,
because there are
some losses that remind you
why some things in our past
are better off left in the holes
we buried them in.

NOVEMBER

*She & I*

She and I will always live like wolves,
competing for space in the wilderness
between your heart and your mind.

She will have one, I will have the other;
together we take turns,
pretend like both is victory.

I wait for the day I stop trading my voice
for howls in the night
and stop confusing you for the moon.


\-     *to ravage alone is better than to share*

It's 1 in the afternoon
and you're still paralyzed and reclusive
in the comfort of your bed,
staring at the lapse of time
as the minutes
stretch into hours,
hours into days,
and just like that
you forget what it's like to
feel the sunlight on your skin.

I don't know how to turn sadness into fashion
like the charming way cool girls do.
All I know is that when it hits,
it feels like a hundred different aches
throbbing all at once.
The sadness is obsidian and relentless,
a dark substance flowing endlessly
absorbing any faint light of courage.

It's falling one hundred fifty meters
down into the trenches,
out of range for anyone to hear you.
You manipulate your mind to process
helplessness into contentment,
and so you say, in the face of darkness,

*"This isn't so bad. I think I'll make a home out of you."*

*A Betting Man*

If you want to be safe, choose her:
she will chew her food
thirty times before she swallows,
lock all the doors twice,
and avoid danger
in every possibility.
It was her carefulness you fell in love with
because you needed reliability,
a safe place to rest your heavy porcelain on.

If you want comfort, choose her:
even on your worst days
she will know all the right words to say,
swathe you in her cashmere tenderness,
and sing hymns of praise
so that every time you wake up
it will feel like Sunday morning.
What you wanted was worship
so she scathed her knees
on the floor for you,
all for the sake of blind faith
without a heaven to promise her.

If you want consistency, choose her:
with her love there is no bad weather
only clear, cerulean skies,
no arbitrary storms
that will leave you with empty hands
in its aftermath.

But if you choose to gamble
with probability
and love *me* instead,
I can promise you this:
you will be tiptoeing at the edge
of cliffs for me, looming at the bottom,
paralyzed by the unsettling awareness of your heartbeat,


because a hellish love like mine is worth
all the danger you've ever missed out on.

*Stay*

A neurotic part of me thinks that I don't deserve anything good. Some lovers were transparent and honest with their inability to commit while others felt more deceiving. Sometimes, the men, came with the stamina and intention to stay, but eventually grew weary towards the end. With this kind of history, it's difficult to believe that a deeply flawed person like myself could have more to offer in love than someone with less problems, less tribulations. To live in constant winter would be to grow tired of the cold no matter how much you romanticize the season. Other women felt like the month of June. I hope someone with patience will come along and endure my winter long enough to see my summer.

*Collateral Damage*

He could not heal
so he shared his pain
with other lovers who had
no desire to have it.

*Crazy*

Say my name
and watch as his eyes
divert to the floor.
You can almost see it;
a montage of all the times
I've ever caused him
distress and trouble
like I am the succubus
that haunts.

What a cowardly way
to place blame
and refuse responsibility.

Funny how catastrophe
struck us both
but we tell
the same story
with different villains.

*Picking Dahlias*


For you, my body was a dahlia.
I spent most nights
ripping off my tattered petals
to prove that I was pretty enough
to be pulled from my roots
and be kept for yourself,
just to die by your bed.

If only I was patient
with loving myself
perhaps
I would have been a garden
to someone else.

*Infertility*

The beautiful things our love could create
but what is against us
is our time

and fate.

*Hues*

The dark colors leak,
spilling through,
they bleed,
and seep
through prettier hues.

Love trickles a scorned crimson,
brushstrokes of black and blue,
painting a picture
that brings me back
to unkind memories of you.

THE ENTIRE ERA,
ALTHOUGH HEARTBREAKING,
SOMEHOW BURIED ITSELF
DEEP INTO THE PORES
OF MY MEMORY FOREVER.

IT'S A TIME THAT
I OFTEN REPRESS, BUT
I LIKE TO REVISIT
EVERY ONCE IN AWHILE

*Palace of Versailles*

My body is not a place to desecrate.
I mistrust any man who is not grateful for the privilege of
entering.

Do you know how long it took for me to restore
all that you have vandalized?
How I am now afraid of another man
turning marble corridors into ruins?
How you swung from chandeliers?
You walked through my gardens and set
a thriving beauty on fire.


Because of you, I found comfort in isolation,
estranged myself from intimacy
until vines grew along the walls.

*One Last Dance*

Underneath a willow tree
a small dahlia blossoms,

By September,
she dances one last time
before her death in autumn.

MARCH

*Toxic Love*

There is a kind of love that is doomed from the start: you will love the wrong person until fate decides when you both will meet the sad demise of a brutal ending. In the last duration of time, you will frantically empty the water out to keep the love floating above water.

But the healthy kind of love will never give you this anxiety. A good lover is dedicated and strong enough to overcome any complications. The foundation is strong, and that idea alone keeps your mind and heart still.

*Haze*

He has paper thin skin
and veins that bulge like
turnpikes on a road map.
I follow them down
with my fingertips,
highways leading nowhere.

Sunlight shines upon
his face,
thick lashes
casting strange
shadows onto his cheeks.

10 am on a Saturday
brings a quiet haze
that's best for loving,
because only when he
was unaware and dreaming
could I see him in his purest form.

Coming out of the dark woods and finding true love
inspired me to believe that good things - beautiful things -
can happen.

By believing that and cutting ties with the lovers who were
not meant for me, I unknowingly created space for fate to
do its magic.

-    *let him go*

*Open Doors*


What I've learned is this:
love is not a concrete prison,
it is a home
with open doors.

I'm still learning
how to watch you leave
with faith that you will always
come back
weary
and
happy to see me.

IT'S YOU. IT'S ALWAYS GONNA BE YOU.

*Magnolias*

He feels wholesome and safe, pure like my childhood.
He once told me how as a child, he'd climb the
highest point of a magnolia tree and pick the most
fragrant, blossomed flower to bring back to his
mother. That is just like his love for me today;

fearless and sacrificial.

Take heed of women like me,
for it is my hex
that allows me to live inside you
long after our farewells
have been said.

The power of resurgence
upon my lips that awakens you
every morning.

I am the rustle
of bare branches
chilling you to the bone.

My body,
the silk cobwebs
that confine you to me.
You are just a paper doll,
you call it

*spellbound*

I call it

*power.*

*How lucky I am*
*that your lips are no longer just a*
*mid-afternoon day dream*

*but now,*
*perceptible by touch,*
*and an authentic place to rest my love.*

APRIL

*Orion's Belt*

A milky canvas
speckled with constellations
of freckles,

but I only ever saw you
when you'd pass through
once every hundred years
as a spectacle in the sky,
for your spirit was
far too big
to be earthbound.

You became something
I was forced to admire
from far away.


-     *and each time,*
*it gets harder and harder to look up*

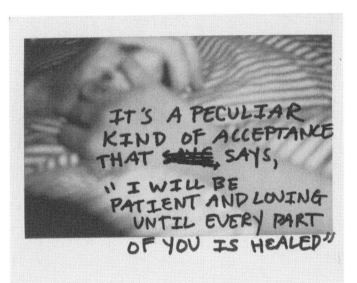

*Koi No Yokan*

Our eyes met for the first time and in that moment, I was stuck in a stillness.
There was a poignant feeling in my heart telling me that although the timing was off, somewhere down the line, the cosmos will listen to my wishes and bring us to each other when we are both ready.

I told God, "If you are real, prove it to me."

So here we are, my love.
Now look at us.
Look at all that the cosmos have done for you and me.

> *You will always be the sweetest victory,*
> *my favorite gift.*

## Jealousy

I'd be lying
if I said that I am the only one
who sees your light.
I am just afraid of other women finding refuge in its
warmth.

I know they see sienna skin
shining molten gold in the summer,
and a jawline that suggests a mouth
big enough to swallow me whole but never would.

But do they see heavy hands,
rough and callous
from building yourself a home
that your father never once step foot in?

Or chili-spiced lips,
red and swollen
from kissing me?

What
exactly
do they see?

You cannot possibly
look as beautiful to them
as you do to me.

*Weather in New England*


Morning slowly leaked
through the curtains like molasses
with the onshore breeze carrying
the sweet petrichor of light rain through windows.

My sister told me,
"If you like the weather, wait five minutes.
If you *don't* like the weather, wait five minutes"

there are lessons on changeability
that the rain can teach us.

*Star Crossed*

Tell me,
do you believe in God?
A natural semblance of things?
An architect
designing intricate details
of our future?

Or do you think life
is rather just a lesson in fluidity?
And each time
we fall in love
or cry on bathroom floors
they are just
the consequences
that adapted
to our own decisions?

Tell me,
for I must know
who is responsible;
to whom do I owe
my debt of gratitude
for aligning the stars
and orchestrating the cosmic mess
that brought you to me?

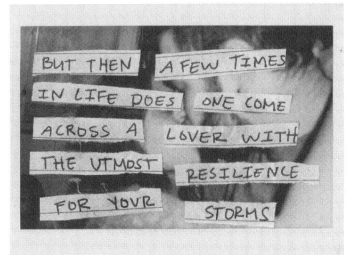

BUT THEN A FEW TIMES IN LIFE DOES ONE COME ACROSS A LOVER WITH THE UTMOST RESILIENCE FOR YOUR STORMS

*As Calm, As Dangerous*

You treat my softness the way you underestimate rivers;
dipping your fingertips in me without regard for what may
lie beneath the depths. But even rivers turn into merciless
oceans that submerge and drown anything it desires. Do
not let my gentle streams fool you into swallowing you
whole.

*Prisms*

There is terror in your heart
that another woman's light could dim your own
so you lived in darkness,

but imagine instead
if we treated each other
like prisms held against
the light,
splashing our colors
onto all those around us.


*- may we as women light the way for each other*

*Home*

Before you, the only kind of love my heart ever knew was the kind that felt as if I had been traveling far through merciless oceans and unforgiving terrains for cities I have never seen.

Like the boy who used to only come around in the summer and use my body, seeking thrills at the greatest heights, and who's sugar spun sweetness left me dizzy and aching by September.

He was Coney Island.

Or like the star-crossed girl I met, opaque as cabernet, who, after time, I could run my fingers down every frayed page of her secrets right down to her deepest yearning. Her cup of café noir leaving clumsy rings onto my memory.

She was Paris.


But then there was you.

You were dirty sneakers by the door and an unmade bed, lilacs and letters on the nightstand. Loving you was a comforting familiarity after years of strange cities, and suddenly, I began to feel homesick anywhere else.

WOODSON ST.

*The Color Yellow*

In the summer sun,
you were canary yellow;
a good omen,
a sign of better days ahead.

On the coldest nights,
you were yellow gold;
your flame flickering
and casting shadows,
mystery and lust colliding.

When spring arrived,
you were lemon yellow,
always making nectar out of
life's acerbic humor.

Your magic is in the way
you exist to me in every season
even when you're gone.

*Love Spell*

I casted a love spell
the night I gave my body to you,
and that is why loneliness
now feels like poisonous pins
throughout your entire body.

*"but love is not magic,"* you said
*"love is a choice."*
That's when I learned
that love is not a cosmic trance
or a temporary state of feeling;


it is a constant decision.

It will be the summer
we walk along the rocky shore
and count all the shades of blue.
On the horizon,
the vermillion sun
sinks into the cobalt ocean,

and as the smell of salt and iodine
fills our lungs,
I will remember how every heartache
brought me to this view,
and how our legs walked voyages
to bring us here
to find this exact moment.


\-     *everything will make sense
and you will be okay*

*Dream of Me*

You rolled over in your sleep and held me close. The warmth of your hands felt like velveteen on the curves of my hips. I never knew how someone could adore me so much that they can't help but show it even in a state of unconscious.

I'm glad that I didn't allow my past experiences with love influence me to pass on a love like this. I was brave enough to not allow fear cheat me out of living a life with you.

And, now,
my lips do not quiver
when I say these words:

*I love you.*

*A girl is a garden;*
*take your time,*
*there is much to see.*

*Some parts sun-soaked,*
*other parts,*
*dark,*
*forgotten.*

*I cupped the water in my hands*
*to carry it with me as far as I could go,*
*and when it slipped through my fingers*
*I punished myself for not being more careful,*
*more graceful.*

*There is a kind of love that feels the same.*
*If it is not meant to go far,*
*leave it behind.*

*All you ever need is yourself.*

*Duality*

They still say your name and expect me to say awful things like hatred should come to me instinctually for all that you have done to me. Yet, I find it strange that I am stumbling over my animosity to find any bit of tenderness left.

Because I cannot mention how your hands are capable of violence without also mentioning its gentleness, the malice without the benevolence.

And all the states in between.

I'd never tell you
that my biggest fear
is to watch adoration
drain from your eyes.
I hope you never struggle to remember
all the reasons why you are here.

I hope you love me at sixty-five
the same way you did when I was
twenty-two,
when my hair was long enough
to brush against my elbows
and the future was mysterious
and thrilling.

I hope consistency
does not bore you
and that, throughout all
life's tribulations,
I was always the one thing
that was refuge from tragedy.

*Bergamot*

This morning, I sat next
 to a lady on a train.
She wafted the smell
of bergamot
like the perfume my
mother used to wear
in winter,
and it brought me back
to falling asleep
on her chest.

Nostalgia is a spirit
in another realm
that wandered too far,
got lost,
and found itself
playing as a familiar song
in a grocery store.
There I am
comparing apples
for the least bruises,
and then suddenly
time stops.

This is the dangerous kind of yearning,
a poignant feeling,
detaching you from
the world entirely.

*Say Your Name*

Make them say your name
the way your mother
intended it to sound,
regardless of how difficult it might be for them;
regardless of how they
stumble upon vowels
or put emphasis
in all the wrong places.

They might wrap their tongues around it,
gauge to see how sour it tastes to them,
and they might spit it out or
add some sugar
to help it go down,

but your culture is
not what they can't swallow,
your culture is not poison
in their mouths.

*Bourbon*

She had a spirit like bubbles in champagne,
effervescent and rose gold.
The saccharine of her apricot lips and skin reminded you
of the honeysuckles you picked in your childhood.
That was her on Sunday mornings.

On Friday night, she was bourbon, the last golden inch in
your glass; hard to love, disdainful, and bitter.
Too strong for your sunny afternoons, you saved her for
the night time when your demons crept through windows
and intrusive thoughts seeped through the walls like
curious ghosts.

For you knew nothing or no one else could numb you the
same way as she could.

*Equinox*

I was born on the day
of an autumnal equinox,
when the day is amber
and night, sapphire.

A time of
change
and a time of
balance.

When the light of the
libra sun
illuminates the auburn
of earl grey
in the morning
or the terracotta sand dunes
in a lover's eyes
until the full harvest moon
leaks a celestial beam
into quiet bedrooms.

There is a bewitching beauty
that autumn brings,
a theatrical show,
until nature rebirths again
through flowing rivers in spring.

*Flora*

A blood orange sun in June
rushed away by light showers
for a sweet affair in bloom.

*Twilight*

We walk hand in hand as the last few minutes of sunlight turn into twilight. I identify every wildflower we come across and, for a moment, we allow our worries to melt away like we have all the time in the world.

*Whole*

I don't want to
always see perfect.
Sometimes I want to see
jealous
and enraged,
vulnerable
and scared.

Because when I
want someone
I must have
all of them.
So don't try and be faultless,
just give me honesty.

*Head in the Clouds*

She has
crowded teeth,
her mother's cheekbones,
and a gleam of mischief in her eyes,

her father's contagious laugh,
and the insufferable need to give
and take love.

There is a juxtaposition about her;
a delicate femininity like a perfume bottle
with just a subtle hint of danger like weaponry.

CUTE BUT PSYCHO

*Wild*

I watch him breathe underneath me as I
bring him to a sudden hysteria when
I find what makes him come closer to the edge.

We try things that have never been done to me
as he praises the wild side
that we both know
he has created.

*Libra Dream Lover*

Ruled by Venus,
Goddess of Love.
I know this to be true
because nothing makes me feel
more powerful than
using love as a velvet whip.

God was confused
with my creation;
gave me a July soul
in a September body,
and a birth day
during the time of year
when cold weather
creeps in the air
just as soon as I fall in love
with the Summer sun.
Maybe this is why I am
predisposed to accepting change
as if they are nothing more than just seasons.

The growth that the changing seasons
demand of me pains me unbearably
but,
still,
I must
bloom.

*For Mothers with Difficult Daughters*

My mother
has the beauty of a
basilica,
too holy to touch
with dirty hands
and too sacred
to pollute with noise.
It was her stoic silence
that made her seem like she was made
out of marble and gold.
She wasn't like the women
my father liked to photograph.
They were all abandoned homes
with boarded windows,
a place where wayward men
come to stay and leave as they please.
I think my Father gets confused sometimes.

My mother is not
warm and American
like cherry pie,
or like your tv sitcom mother.
Those women were always gentle and forgiving.
Instead, she led with much more logic than with affection.
For instance, the first time I cried over a boy she didn't tell
me that everything was going to be okay. She told me this
feeling will happen a hundred more times, and she was
right.

Maybe her love was just more practical.

Maybe it was not tenderness that I needed after all,
because now there is nothing a man can do to me that my
father hasn't already done to her heart,
yet her eyes have stayed dry for thirty years.

There is strength in that.

I want to say "Mom, I love you."
but the words desperately cling onto the end of my tongue,
climb back, and buries itself until it's safe again in the
back of my mind.

Maybe we weren't what we asked for, but we are what we
have.

- *what I mean to say is this: thank you for giving me
  this heavy armor to protect me from catastrophe
  whenever it strikes again and again and again.*

We often talk about
the little death that we experience
when someone chooses to walk away,
how to villainize someone
and hold them responsible for the
hole in our hearts,

but nobody talks about how it feels
to hold the knife,
how it feels to be the one to
must abandon,
or how the words
*"I know I promised you this, but I'm sorry"*
tastes like vinegar.

We don't talk about the only
 two options one must sometimes weigh out:
*to live in constant misery*
*or to choose life,*
how choosing the latter
is sometimes the only way out
of rock bottom for them,
or even how to apologize for the decision.

The lovelorn will eventually heal,
but the heartbreakers must live life
with the haunting consequences
of the decisions that we make.

*Four Horsemen*

The one night I will always remember is when he and I
secluded ourselves from our friends and sat in a bathroom
on a cold, tiled floor. We talked about our childhood and
our favorite Stephen King novels as the chemicals *dripped,
dripped, dripped,* in the back of our throats. I remember
my mouth tasting like batteries and my lips going numb.
There, I had my first alcoholic drink, a Four Horsemen,
and as the world began to tilt I remember feeling a peculiar
kind of stillness. Warm, fuzzy. I felt present and
untroubled by the anxieties of where I should have been
instead. I was okay. I was here, and the air was thick with
a serendipitous magic that felt as if I was exactly where I
was supposed to be.

## 25

Here's the most difficult part of being twenty-five: it's okay to face an existential crisis every day of the week when you're nineteen; the angst is almost instinctual to the confusion and pressures of youth. You aren't *supposed* to know all the answers. But at twenty-five, it then becomes sad and alarming. The slow ascend into adulthood turns into a dark purgatory. It's the idea of *"not only do I still have this scary vastness living in my chest, but now I'm responsible for it."*

You become strangers to those who still know all your secrets. You will see old lovers and feel the weight of remorse because intimacy was a privilege that no longer belongs to you.

Still, there is a light that signifies hope and it will teach you this: not everyone is meant to serve as a pretty poem, a lesson, or a story to be told. They are here to cope with us for the time being and we will move on.

*- the world is not permanent herself, forever is an illusion.*

*Sea of Trees*

The Japanese say that
the Aokigahara forest
is so thick with foliage that
the ones who wander will
tie red strings around the trees
just in case they change their minds
and want to turn back around.

A frustrating thing about
a person who struggles
with both loving loneliness
and hating loneliness
is that they are never happy.
Depression and anxiety
organically twist like trees, trying hard
to reach the sunlight.
Their roots wind across the treacherous
forest floor making it harder to climb out of the
darkness.
If you are not careful, you could get lost forever.
I think how life has ended for me many times
but I fought my way out of the wilderness to say that
I am still here.
That subtle gleam of hope carries me through
the chasms of emptiness.
Love came to me when I was not searching for it,
and when I found passion, it gave me the momentum
to keep going.

There is a promise of better days ahead,
and you must trust it like the red string that leads you
back to home.

## Live, Laugh, Suffer

Growing up has been all about finding self-identity and being my most authentic self. It's the first time I didn't feel like I had to listen to the fake "live, laugh, love" inspiration that people talk about all the time. Self-love was a lot harder than what people said it'd be.

I had to really reach into the dark ether and pull out the worst parts of myself, look at it in the monstrous face and tell it, *"I have finally identified you and I am not afraid, nor am I going to hate myself because of you any longer. I am going to nurture you until you're healed so that I may become the best possible version of myself."*

So, I started becoming more conscious of other people's emotions; I looked at strangers in the face and imagined them all as their inner child. I was more careful with my words, and more mindful of their vulnerability. I was suddenly gentler, more understanding. That was empathy.

Then, there were other days when I had to pick and choose my battles more wisely. I called for bloodshed with my mouth, became a wolf with a lifeless carcass in my jaw…but only when necessary. I have been overshadowed and seen as docile too many times in the past, to the point people forgot how quickly my anger can stop ocean tides and that I, too, am just as powerful. Some people needed to be reminded of that. That was inner strength.

Last, there were times when the best form of revenge was no revenge at all. That was the most obvious indication that I had truly grown; I was so selfish, so immersed in my own care for myself that I had no energy left to give to my enemies. I had no personal vendetta towards whoever hurt me in the past. I wanted to preserve the energy instead of wasting it on trying to convince someone out of their one-dimensional idea of me. The last version they have of me is of a person that no longer exists, and they will never be able to know the better version of myself. When I wanted to dismantle an enemy, I simply lived.

That was apathy.

It's not about bath bombs or expensive skin care. You can't spray rose water on your problems and pretend like your toxic habits are floral and pretty. It's about fixing yourself at your own pace. It's about accepting, but not tolerating, your worst parts. Because if you are going to grow, let it be honest.


-    *things to know by twenty-five*

I.

You will be misunderstood by many but, eventually, you will meet the right people and it will finally give you the sense of acceptance and belonging that you've yearned for your entire life. Give your love to people who are ready to give theirs to you. Don't take their patience and love for granted. Hold these people close. If not physically, then always in your heart and infinitely in your memories.

II.

You will spend a significant amount of time figuring out who you are, as you try on different clothes and personalities, until you come to realize that who you are is not a fixed state. You are constantly evolving, a multi-faceted gemstone with a full spectrum of different colors and personas.

III.

Leave yourself behind. All the different women you once were. Don't allow the fear of change keep you from growing.

IV.

You will eventually become comfortable with being your most authentic self. You'll grow tired of all the masks you've been so devoted to relying on to feel beautiful. Learning who you really are is scary at first but, in time, you will get to know her, and you will love her. It will feel like a sweet relief because there is no more pressure to be anybody else.

## V.

Your relationship with other women should be tender and supportive, not competitive. Sisterhood is all that we have, after all.

## VI.

When it's time to leave, leave in a quiet and merciless manner. Don't fight what fate is attempting to devise. Love will find its way back to you. Through unforgiving storms, your heart holds the most resilience.

## VII.

Nostalgia is a liar that convinces you that the past is better than the present. It's easy, much too easy, to forget that the future holds just as much beauty.

ATLANTA, GA

# Index

*Acknowledgments*

I would like to thank my mother for conditioning me into believing that women are strong enough to endure anything that life may throw at us. My father, for believing in me with every ounce of that big heart of his, and for also constantly reminding me that life really is a beautiful thing. My sister, for the wisdom and sisterhood. Thank you for seeing the passionate spark in me.

My friends, for the memories, stories, and lessons that I will carry with me throughout this life. Thank you for opening your arms to me, thank you for letting me experience life with you, thank you for the conversations on bathroom floors at 4 am. Without your friendship, I don't think these stories would be as, uh, colorful. Along with that, a huge thank-you to the readers that have supported my writing since the very beginning. Thank you endlessly for believing in me throughout all these years, convincing me that this book would ever be possible. I can only continue to share these stories with you in hopes that you find yourselves in them and feel a sense of comfort and positivity.

Most importantly, I owe a special thank-you to all the lovers in the past that have acted as the fuel and inspiration to my stories. You have helped me become the woman neither of us thought I'd ever be. May I tell my stories honestly and not with bitterness.

*About the Author*

Jen Handoko is a writer and poet born in Indonesia and raised in Atlanta, Georgia. Writing at an early age, she found scribbling in notebooks to be a therapeutic, healthy way to express herself. Through personal experiences, she aims to bring awareness to domestic violence and mental health through creative writing. Jen Handoko lives in Atlanta, Georgia with her lover and their dogs.

photography: hanae clark

For more information, visit www.jenhandoko.com

*Equinox*

ISBN-10: 1987675606
ISBN-13: 978-1987675603

22761905R00099

Printed in Great Britain
by Amazon